Paint·a· Quilt PATTERNS

Marie Monteith Sturmer

Located in Paducah, Kentucky, the American Quilter's Society (AQS) is dedicated to promoting the accomplishments of today's quilters. Through its publications and events, AQS strives to honor today's quiltmakers and their work and to inspire future creativity and innovation in quiltmaking.

EDITOR: LINDA BAXTER LASCO
GRAPHIC DESIGN: AMY CHASE
COVER DESIGN: MICHAEL BUCKINGHAM
PHOTOGRAPHY: CHARLES R. LYNCH

Library of Congress Cataloging-in-Publication Data
Sturmer, Marie Monteith.
    Paint-a-quilt patterns / by Marie Monteith Sturmer.
      p. cm.
    Summary: "Learn the trace and transfer technique and detailed instructions for coloring in the shapes by dry-brushing, pouncing, streaking, and circular motions with acrylic paints. Patterns can be used for applique, embroidery, and scrapbooking, and are useful for stenciling on walls, wood, and craft projects"-- Provided by publisher.
    Includes bibliographical references.
    ISBN 1-57432-920-0
    1. Quilting--Patterns. 2. Stencil work. I. Title.

TT835.S755 2007
746.46'041--dc22
                        2006036131

Additional copies of this book may be ordered from the American Quilter's Society, PO Box 3290, Paducah, KY 42002-3290; 800-626-5420 (orders only please); or online at www.AmericanQuilter.com. For all other inquiries, please call 270-898-7903.

Dedication

To my dear husband, Ralph, for all his patient support

Acknowledgments

I am very grateful to Ellen Allen, who has been so faithful and willing to transpose my thoughts onto her computer.

Brenda Sheldon has proved to me that my stencil quilts can look beautiful with her machine quilting. Thank you, Brenda.

Special thanks to my son, Jim, for providing me with the wonderful background music of Mozart, Beethoven, and Bach that has filled my studio for endless hours.

Contents

Introduction

At a gathering of local quiltmakers at the Park Place Hotel in Traverse City, Michigan, some years ago, the meeting ended with Show and Tell. One woman displayed a beautiful stencil-painted quilt she had found in a chest of drawers bought at an auction. What a find it was!

The quilt is a wonderful example of a medallion-style quilt, hand-stenciled on a wholecloth with very fine hand quilting. The quilt was in excellent condition because it had never been completed and used. The only thing lacking was the hem at the edges of the quilt. The lovely rounded fruit, low-footed urns, and assorted flower arrangements all painted with dark colors are just the kinds of subjects a stencil quiltmaker would have used in the 1820s. The open rose border, however, does not quite match the style or painting technique used for the other motifs. It is possible that another quilter painted the design on the border. From the quality of the stitches, it appears one person did all of the quilting (photo 1).

How well I remember that day. Thoughts of that beautiful stenciled quilt just haunted me. That was the day my decision was made to become a stencil quiltmaker. Many years of teaching stenciling projects to my art students prepared me for things to come—so many days, so many ideas, so many quilts. My collection of stencil-painted quilts has grown, and now it's time to share them.

I am truly a stenciler. I enjoy making the decision for the inclusion of "bridges" within the design, the precise measuring that must occur for a successful layout, and the real fun that comes with the painting. I like the way stencil painting does things in a hurry. If you aspire to be a stencil quiltmaker, you are not alone, and I have full instructions to take you through each step for creating a stencil quilt of your own.

This collection includes a floorcloth with the same stencil design as used on a quilt. A floorcloth may spark an idea for your next quilt project. Sometimes all it takes is a change in a color scheme or a novel arrangement of a design.

If there's a design that appeals to you, make a photocopy and try some enlargements to see if a different size appeals to you more. To make a design even more original, try redrawing different motifs to develop something that really satisfies you.

Photo 1. FLOWER URNS WITH OPEN ROSE BORDER, 67" x 84", cotton wholecloth quilt, stencil-painted design. Hand-quilted circa 1820, possibly made in Michigan, quiltmaker unidentified (privately owned).

This is a book full of wonderful stencil designs. Making your own decisions as to how the design of the quilt will develop is a good start on becoming a creative quiltmaker. All the small stencil patterns found throughout the quilt collection were bigger when I used them and can be enlarged in an instant on a copy machine. I am sure you will find a special design waiting for you.

For those who like the stencil designs but might not want to cut and paint a stencil, I have introduced the trace and transfer technique. It is an easy way to reproduce a design on fabric with only a simple drawing method. Several examples of this technique are shown. These wall quilts have been inspired by a full-sized, stencil-painted quilt having similar stencil designs. All of the stencil designs can be adapted to this technique.

Making a wall quilt is a good way to become familiar with the drawing technique. Full instructions are given in the Making a Trace and Transfer Quilt section starting on page 16. Painting on fabric is always a one-of-a-kind work of art, no matter which technique is followed.

Experiment with color by using some of the ideas listed in the Thoughts on Color section starting on page 22. A variety of stenciling props (see page 9) can be used to produce interesting faux-printed fabrics. Try all the options until you are comfortable with what you have learned … and have fun!

Making a Stenciled Quilt

Before you start painting, I'd like to explain some basic stenciling methods and vocabulary. I've included some thoughts on design considerations and a discussion of color and color combinations.

Stencil Talk

Stencils allow you to easily repeat a design pattern over and over. Most stencils are made from Mylar®. It is available in 8" x 10" sheets from quilt and craft stores and in larger sheets from architecture and craft suppliers. A gauge of 5 mil is easy to cut.

Stencil designs can be scanned into your computer and printed directly onto your template material. Be sure to use the correct material depending on whether you are printing on an ink jet or laser printer.

The narrow strips of stencil material between the open holes of the stencil are called "bridges." Bridges are spacers of stencil material that give support to the open portions of the design. Wide bridges give a bold feeling to the design. Thin bridges give a light, delicate feeling. Staying with one bridge size throughout a design establishes unity and rhythm, especially when the design is repeated many times.

Stencil patterns can be used for more than just stenciling. When tracing a pattern to be used for trace and transfer freehand painted projects, the trace lines are drawn through the center of the bridges, producing a pattern that still has its original characteristics.

A copy machine can be used to enlarge or reduce patterns. Ask an attendant at the copy center to help you, because he or she uses a sizing scale that will compute the exact size desired.

Any of these stencil designs can be digitized and used for embroidery machines or as needlework designs.

Stencil Painting Techniques

The most common stencil painting technique is called "pouncing." An up-and-down pouncing motion of the brush creates a stippled effect (fig. 1). Streaking and stroking the brush produces a variety of painted stripes and can create a feeling of motion (figs. 2 and 3). A circular motion of the brush creates a swirling stroke and is a simple way to shade colors (fig. 4).

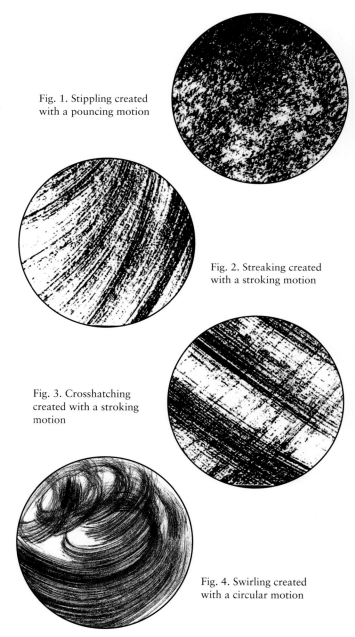

Fig. 1. Stippling created with a pouncing motion

Fig. 2. Streaking created with a stroking motion

Fig. 3. Crosshatching created with a stroking motion

Fig. 4. Swirling created with a circular motion

A smooth texture is achieved with evenly applied color. It will look slick or shiny. A rough texture comes from unevenly applied color with stippling, swirling, or streaking brush strokes.

Stenciling Props

Stenciling props, such as chicken wire, hardware cloth, plastic onion bag (stretched in an embroidery hoop), window screen, or extruded metal, provide a way to make a variety of textures and create an amazing likeness to printed fabric.

Place a stenciling prop over the stencil opening and apply the paint with the pouncing method (figs. 5–10).

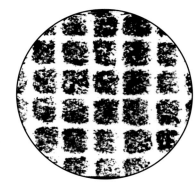

Fig. 7.
¼" hardware cloth

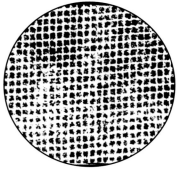

Fig. 8.
Wire window screen

Fig. 5.
Plastic onion bag

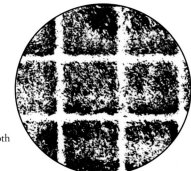

Fig. 9.
½" hardware cloth

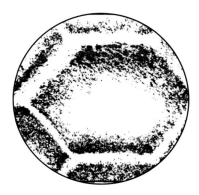

Fig. 6.
Chicken wire

Fig 10.
Extruded metal

Stenciling Shield

A single stencil can be used for painting more than one color by using a stenciling shield to block out adjacent openings. Trace the outline of the stenciling shield pattern on a sheet of Mylar and cut it out (fig. 11). To use the stenciling shield, select the best-fitting notch or curve to cover adjacent openings to prevent an unwanted mix of colors.

Fig. 11. Stenciling shield pattern

Paint-a-Quilt Supplies

Fabric

100 percent cotton

Work Accessories

Plastic container lid for palette
Ruler and yardstick
45-degree/90-degree triangle for squaring up lines
Iron and ironing board
Blue, water-soluble fabric marking pen
Masking tape
Water jar

Stencil Brushes

A typical stencil brush is round with short, stiff bristles. Brushes come in ¼", ⅜", ½", ⅝", and 1" sizes. A 1" brush is good for large stencil openings. Flat artist oil brushes size #2, #4, or larger, work well for freehand painting on fabric.

Stencils

Mylar (frosted on one side)
Blue painter's masking tape
Black permanent felt-tip pen or laundry marker
Single-edged razor blades or utility knife
Small sharp-pointed embroidery scissors
½" thick glass with masking-taped edges for a cutting surface (a 9" x 12" piece works well)
Fingernail polish remover
Transparent tape

Stencil Paint

Acrylic paint that comes in squeeze bottles is more fluid and easier to work with than artist-brand acrylic paints. They're available at craft stores.

Decorator acrylic or latex interior or exterior house paint is a good source for specially mixed colors, as are textured craft paints. All paints must be marked permanent.

Stencil Making

Trace or print the stencil design onto the template material. One stencil will be cut for the entire design, even if the design will be painted with more than one color. You'll use the stenciling shield to cover one or more stencil openings when painting a different color in an adjacent opening.

Stencil Cutting Tips

- Place the stencil material on a cutting base of plate glass with taped edges. Tilt your cutting blade at an angle and use only the front tip.
- Hold the blade hand stationary and move the stencil sheet into the cutting blade with the other hand.

- Be careful not to over cut at corners. Slight criss-cross cuts may cause the stencil sheet to rip.
- Use transparent tape to mend a miscut.
- Use a razor blade or craft knife to cut all straight or long flowing stencil lines.
- Cut curved lines and small parts with straight-pointed embroidery scissors after a razor slash has been made in the open part of the design.
- To make smooth clockwise cuts with scissors, hold them on the underside of the stencil sheet. For counterclockwise cuts, hold the scissors on the top of the stencil sheet.
- Cut small areas of the stencil first and the larger openings last.
- Make dots with a paper or leather punch.

Cutting Tip

1. Lay the stencil sheet, frosted side up, over the desired pattern, allowing a 1" margin of Mylar around the stencil design.
2. Tape in place with blue painter's tape.
3. Draw the complete pattern outline with a permanent pen.
4. Place an X in the parts to be cut out.
5. Refer to the cutting tips above to cut out the stencil.
6. When cutting is complete, use nail polish remover to clean all pencil marks from the stencil.

Designing Your Quilt

The design may be symmetrical or asymmetrical and should be planned with the idea of being repeated in a harmonious way.

The asymmetrical placement of the flowers within a vertical panel of leaves and stems weaves a novel arrangement in BIG STITCH (fig. 1).

LAUREL ROSE has a classic, symmetrical repetition of the design components in the center, touching each other and creating other designs (fig. 2). The master plan for the quilt started in the center and grew outward. Working from a sketch of what the quilt might be and then letting things fall into place has been my way of creating.

Fig 1. (top) Asymmetrical design: BIG STITCH stencil pattern is on page 66.
Fig. 2. (bottom) Symmetrical design: LAUREL ROSE stencil patterns are on page 70.

The setting of the quilt blocks will dictate the construction and position of the stencil design. A wholecloth quilt may be designed with block patterns and stenciled sashing as an allover design or as a medallion-style quilt with stenciled borders.

Stencil painting for this wholecloth BALTIMORE-STYLE ALBUM quilt began with the red sashing and border motifs (fig. 3). Some of the block patterns and the border leaf designs were inspired by the Sarah and Mary J. Pool album quilts, 1840s, Baltimore, Maryland. Each painted block has some type of embroidery work, and a few blocks are enhanced by pen and ink, an accepted technique for Baltimore quilts.

Fig. 3. Wholecloth quilt in block style. BALTIMORE-STYLE ALBUM stencil patterns are on pages 72–81.

In 1991, when my quilt MICHEGAMEE'S WILD ROSE was placed in the permanent quilt collection of the American Folk Art Museum in New York City, I knew I wanted to have one just like it for my own. With the original set of stencils for the quilt, I reproduced my medallion-style wholecloth Wild Rose quilt (fig. 4).

If you are timid about painting on wholecloth, cut fabric blocks adding a ¼" seam allowance for piecing. CAROLINA LILY is made this way (fig. 5). The foundation for this quilt block design was laid by painting the black

Fig. 4. Medallion-style wholecloth quilt. (MARIE'S) MICHEGAMEE'S WILD ROSE stencil patterns are on pages 52–53.

Fig. 5. Quilt constructed in blocks. CAROLINA LILY stencil pattern is on page 83.

hairpin-like stencils first, creating a symmetrical pattern. The red and green colors become a subordinate feature.

When designing your quilt, make several paper mock-ups of your stencil pattern to try out different repeats and placement ideas. The given motifs can change places when a better idea steps in. Things will work out every time if you measure carefully. The freedom of working this way adds to the joy of quiltmaking.

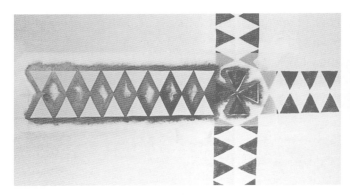

Preparing the Fabric

You will need to prewash your fabric. Fabric paint will not be permanent if you paint over sizing. Press to remove all wrinkles and remove the selvages.

1. Fold the prepared fabric in half, matching the edges and following the fabric grain line. Press the folded edge with a warm iron.
2. Fold the fabric again, matching the folded edges. Press the new fold. This establishes the guidelines.
3. Starting in the center, use a yardstick to measure all the placement lines for the stencils from the horizontal and vertical pressed guidelines.
4. Mark all placement lines with a blue water-soluble fabric marking pen before the painting takes place.

Stencil Painting Set-Up

Stencil painting is a dry-brush technique, which means that very little paint is used on the brush. It is like painting with a slightly dirty brush. You need to work slowly and be alert. Expect the unexpected, but have a positive attitude.

Before you start painting, make sure that all pencil marks have been cleaned from the stencil. The lead could bleed into your paint, making it muddy. You'll need to cover or protect your worktable and keep a jar filled with water nearby to hold used brushes for cleaning later in soap and hot water.

Stencil Painting Sequence

Paint all sashing and borders with the dominant color, beginning in the center of the quilt and working out toward the edges. Paint the outer sashing borders, starting at the corners (fig. 6). Adjustments in the outer borders can be made at the center of the sides. Shifting the stencil and "fudging" a little is the fun part of stenciling.

Fig. 6. All sashing strips are painted first, then the outer sashing borders are painted, starting at the corners.

Arrange and paint stencil block designs between the sashing strips (fig. 7).

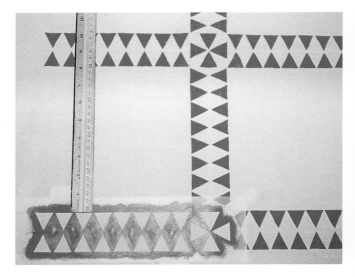

Fig. 7. Stencil block designs are painted, starting with the dominant color.

Stencil Painting Method

Use masking tape to secure the stencil to the fabric. Place a half teaspoon of paint on a palette and work a small amount of paint into the brush. Test on a piece of scrap fabric and work any excess paint onto the scrap fabric.

To paint, move the brush from the stencil sheet into the stencil opening to prevent paint from seeping under the stencil. Always start painting with a light touch, working the paint from light to dark. It is easy to create a dark color by going over the same spot several times, but once it is dark, there is no good method for making it lighter.

Stencil Painting Tips

- Do not allow paint to build up in the brush.
- Use a toothpick to paint in all small dots or lines.
- Frequently lift the stencil off the fabric to check for excess paint on the back. Lay the stencil on paper toweling and rub the surface with another paper towel to remove excess paint from both the front and the back of the stencil.
- It is much easier to re-cut a new, clean stencil than to spend time reclaiming a dirty one.
- Never paint with a wet or partly damp brush because the diluted paint will bleed onto the fabric.
- If you need to use a just-washed brush, use your finger to press the bristles into a dry cellulose sponge to remove all moisture.
- Spray (can) adhesive will hold the stencil in place.

Reverse Painting

When the cut-out material from a stencil opening is used as a template to cover the background fabric, a reverse technique occurs (fig. 8). In SNOWFLAKES the circles of white are painted over the snowflakes, which were cut from folded paper. The paper cutouts hide the blue fabric of the blocks so it is not touched by the paint. This method of stenciling is known as reverse painting.

After Painting

To ensure the lasting beauty of stencils painted on fabrics, the paint must cure. Allow the paint to dry overnight.

Use a damp cloth to remove all the blue pen lines left from the stencil layout pen. Allow the fabric to dry and then heat-set the paint with a hot, dry iron. Press the back first, then press the front with a pressing cloth.

Fig 8. Reverse painting: SNOWFLAKES detail. See instructions for cutting snowflakes on page 67 .

Making a Trace and Transfer Quilt

The trace and transfer method starts with a stencil design but it is drawn differently to produce a line drawing on fabric that looks much like a page from a coloring book. Any stencil design can be adapted to the trace and transfer technique.

This floral motif stencil (fig. 1) has been traced to produce a trace and transfer template (fig. 2). Instead of stencil painting through an opening, the open areas of the drawing are painted with acrylic craft paint and flat artist's oil painting brushes.

Fig. 1. Floral motif stencil

Fig. 2. Floral motif drawn as a trace and transfer pattern

The trace and transfer technique worked very well on this little wall quilt (fig. 3). The perky strawberry vines came off as line drawings, which is unique to this technique. The strawberries were brushed with acrylic craft paint leaving the white fabric to show as shiny highlights.

Fig. 3. Detail of STRAWBERRIES TO EAT, painted with the trace and transfer technique. Stencil pattern is on page 85.

Supplies

- Clear sheets of acetate or plastic, 4 mil thick, available at architecture supply stores. Plastic sheet protectors, available at office supply stores, work as well.
- Smudge-free black carbon paper for light-colored quilt top
- Wax-free, light-colored dressmakers tracing paper for dark-colored quilt top
- Black permanent felt-tip laundry pen
- Selection of artist oil painting brushes, #2, #4, or larger
- Acrylic craft paint
- Blue painter's masking tape
- Blue water-soluble fabric marking pen
- A sturdy blunt pencil for transferring the design

Making the Template

Cut a clear acetate sheet at least 1" larger than the design. Lay the acetate over the design and tape it in place. Trace the full design using a black permanent marker, drawing through the center of any bridges. This completes the template. Study the pattern for spots from which to measure and draw placement lines on your prepared fabric.

Preparing the Fabric

You will need to prewash your fabric. Fabric paint will not be permanent if you paint over sizing. Press to remove all wrinkles and remove the selvages.

1. Fold the prepared fabric in half, matching the edges and following the fabric grain line. Press the folded edge with a warm iron.
2. Fold the fabric again, matching the folded edges. Press the new fold. This establishes the guidelines.

3. Starting in the center, use a yardstick to measure all the placement lines for the stencils from the horizontal and vertical pressed guidelines.

4. Mark placement lines with a blue water-soluble fabric marking pen.

Transferring the Design

1. Place the fabric on a hard, smooth surface. (Paint and black marker may bleed through the fabric.)

2. Place the acetate template pattern over the designated area on the fabric.

3. Tape only one side in place.

4. Slip the carbon or wax-free tracing paper under the template.

5. Tape down all sides of the template.

6. Trace over the design, pressing hard with a blunt pencil to transfer the lines to the fabric.

7. Reposition the template and repeat steps 2–6 to complete the entire quilt top design.

8. Retrace all lines directly on the fabric, using a black permanent felt-tip pen.

Painting the Design

Study the color wheel and the color combinations to select your color scheme. (See the discussion of color on page 22). Paint the open spaces of the transferred design with artist's oil painting brushes.

Allow the paint to dry overnight. Use a damp cloth to remove all the blue pen lines left from the stencil layout plan and allow the fabric to dry before heat-setting the paint.

Heat-set the color with a hot, dry iron. Press the back first, then press the front with a pressing cloth. Retrace all the black pen lines to make them stand out.

Shark's Teeth Edging

The Origin of Shark's Teeth

Throughout the history of quiltmaking, quilters have often felt a close association to a special pattern or a particular technique, claiming it as their own. Thus, many times an established name has been changed to reflect the quiltmaker's endeavors. My own experience with prairie points is an example of this.

One day, when my grandson came to my house for a special nap time, we engaged in our ritual in which I allowed him to go into my quilt closet and choose a quilt for the day. His choice was a wholecloth stencil album quilt. When he jumped in bed and I flung the quilt high in the air to cover him, he squealed, "Shark's teeth!" My quaint little prairie point edging now had a new name.

Whether his dreams were of sharks, I do not know, but I do know that the special magic of one of his grandmother's stenciled quilts has always promoted a long, refreshing nap. I am sure he will always remember the shark's teeth of small folded fabric points as the quilt's identifying feature (fig. 1).

Fig. 1. Mexican Rose detail with shark's teeth edging

Instructions for Making Shark's Teeth

The quilt should be quilted before applying the shark's teeth. Leave at least ½" between the quilting stitches and the edge of the quilt.

Measure the Quilt

Divide the dimensions of the quilt length and width in half. You will work with two separate folded strips for each side of the quilt; that is, eight folded strips for the complete quilt edging.

Materials

Fabric
Paper
Cellophane tape
Tape measure
Ruler
Heavy cord or yarn
Iron and ironing surface

Make the Tube

For 1" shark's teeth, cut a strip of fabric 3" wide and twice the length of the quilt edge dimension, plus 6". For larger points, cut wider strips.

1. Fold the fabric strip in half lengthwise with right sides together and press.
2. Measure a length of heavy yarn a little longer than the length of the fabric strip.
3. Place the yarn inside the folded fabric and stitch across the end of the fabric to secure one end of the yarn.
4. Stitch the long, open edges of the folded fabric with a ⅛" seam allowance to make a tube. Keep the yarn within the tube, making sure not to catch it in the seam.
5. Tie the loose end of the yarn to a doorknob and skin the fabric back over the yarn, starting at the stitched end, to turn the fabric to the right side.
6. Press the turned tube flat along the stitched seam edge.

Make Placement Strips

Cut enough 1" wide paper strips to equal the

outside edges of the quilt. Measure the width of the prepared tube. The width will equal the space between the points of the shark's teeth. Make pencil marks along the paper strips at intervals equal to the tube width.

Fold the Shark's Teeth

Folding Tips

The ironing board makes a good work surface.
Folds are made at a 45-degree angle.
Press fabric as it is folded.

Working from the back (folded side) of the points, there are just four steps to perform, as shown in figure 2.

Use a small piece of cellophane tape to secure the fabric points to the paper strip for even spacing. The tape also stabilizes the fabric strip when pinning and stitching the points to the quilt top. Do not stitch through the paper.

Attach the Shark's Teeth

The shark's teeth strip will be stitched only to the quilt top. Fold the batting and backing fabric onto the back of the quilt and pin out of the way.

All eight folded strips should be stitched from the corner so you can make any slight adjustments at the halfway mark where the two folded strips join. The seam of a mitered corner in the final outer border aids in placement of the shark's teeth. Align the edge of the end point with the seam of your mitered border. If your border isn't mitered, mark a temporary line in from the quilt corners at a 45 degree angle and use that to align your shark's teeth.

1. Align the straight edge of the shark's teeth strip with the raw edge of the quilt top, with the folded back of the points facing up and the teeth pointing in toward the quilt (fig. 3).
2. Pin the shark's teeth strip to the edge of the quilt top, starting at the corner and moving toward the center of the quilt.

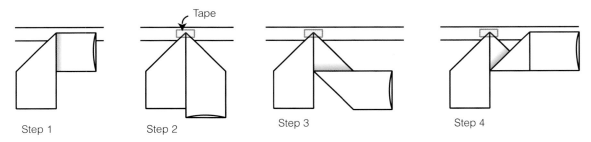

Step 1   Step 2   Step 3   Step 4

Fig. 2. Folding shark's teeth: Complete steps 1 through 4. After folding the strip up in step 4, return to step 2 and continue repeating steps 2 through 4 to the end of the strip.

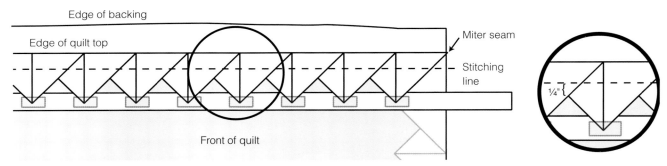

Fig. 3 Sewing the shark's teeth strip to the quilt

3. Sew ¼" from the bottom of the V shape between the points, beginning at the corner of the quilt top.

4. Trim the seam allowance to remove extra bulkiness.

5. Remove the paper strips. Trim any extra fabric from the backing, leaving a ¼" seam allowance. Trim batting if needed.

6. Press the teeth outward from the quilt. Fold the backing fabric over and bring the folded edge to the stitching line and hand finish.

Design Option

To create shark's teeth in an alternating color combination, make the tube by sewing strips of two different colored fabrics together, adding an extra ⅛" of seam allowance to both strips. For example, for 1" points, you would cut two strips, each 1⅝" wide. As the fabric strip is folded into points, the different fabrics will alternate (fig. 4).

Fig. 4. CHRISTMAS SPIDER PLANT detail with alternating shark's teeth

Floorcloths

Any of the stencil designs in this book can be used to create floorcloths. Making floorcloths requires some additional supplies, but the stenciling method is the same.

Water-base paint will shrink canvas about 1" per yard. Oil-base paint will not shrink the canvas. Keep the finished floorcloth flat on the floor by using masking tape "donuts" on the underside of the corners.

Materials

Heavy awning canvas
Carpenter's glue
Palette knife
Large binder clips or jumbo paper clips
Water- or oil-base paint
Acrylic stencil paints
Polyurethane
Paint brushes
Masking tape
Stencils

Floorcloth Method

1. Trim all four sides of the canvas and turn under a 1½" hem.
2. Secure the hem with carpenter's glue, spread evenly with a palette knife, and use jumbo paper clips to hold the hem in place to dry.
3. Paint both sides of the hemmed canvas with several base coats.
4. Stencil paint designs over the base paint.
5. Seal with several coats of polyurethane.

Fig. 1. HOLIDAY HEIRLOOM floorcloth made by the author. With the quilt blocks set on point, the sashing creates a circle; stencil pattern is on page 38.

Thoughts on Color

The color wheel can play an important part in planning colors for a successful quilt (fig. 1).

Many of these stenciled quilts started with traditional quilt block designs, but they're not quite like the originals. I redesigned them by selecting special motifs from old designs and reorganizing them to fit my feeling of creating it my way. Then I selected a color combination of my own.

Study the different color combinations I have used. Then refer to the color wheel to establish your own color scheme (figs. 2–7).

Color Wheel Combinations

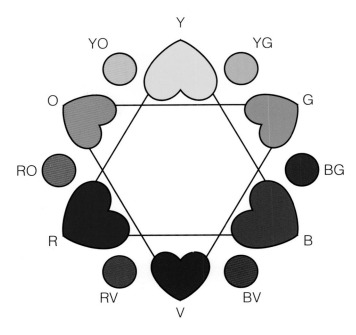

Fig. 1. Color wheel

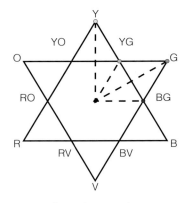

Fig. 2. Analogous: two to four adjacent colors, sometimes called neighboring colors

Primary Colors	Secondary Colors
Red (R)	R + Y = O (Orange)
Yellow (Y)	Y + B = G (Green)
Blue (B)	B + R = V (Violet)

Intermediate Colors

Y + O = YO (Yellow Orange)

Y + G = YG (Yellow Green)

B + G = BG (Blue Green)

B + V = BV (Blue Violet)

R + V = RV (Red Violet)

R + O = RO (Red Orange)

Photo 1. ROB PETER TO PAY PAUL floorcloth with analogous color combination; stencil pattern is on page 87.

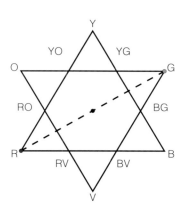

Fig. 3. Complementary: two colors directly opposite each other on the color wheel

Photo 2. Rose Sprigs floorcloth with complementary color combination; trace and transfer patterns are on pages 89–90

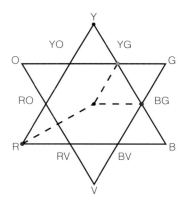

Fig. 4. Split Complementary: three colors, one color and two intermediate colors, on either side of its complementary color

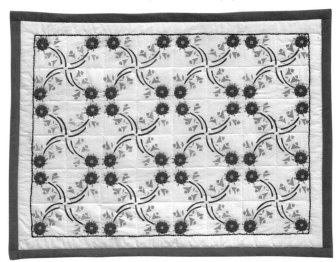

Photo 3. Author's Choice with split complementary color combination of R, YG, BG

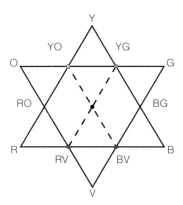

Fig. 5. Double-split Complementary: four colors; the four intermediate colors on either side of two complementary colors

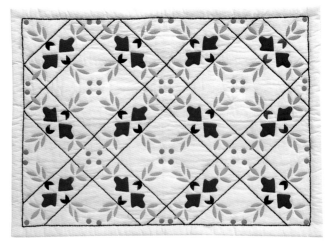

Photo 4. Pineapple Clusters with double-split complementary color combination of YO, YG, RV, and BV; stencil pattern is on page 28

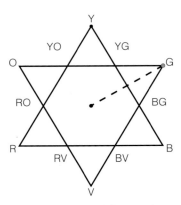

Fig. 6. Monochromatic: one color, different values and intensities

Photo 5. MONOCHROMATIC MELODY with a monochromatic color scheme; patterns are on page 40

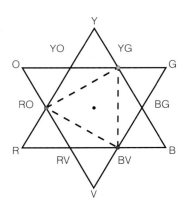

Fig. 7. Triad: three colors plotted on an equilateral triangle on the color wheel

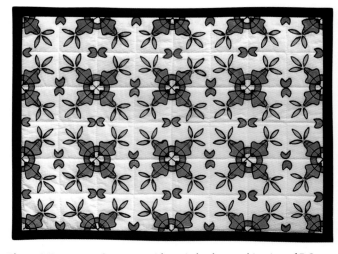

Photo 6. PINEAPPLE CLUSTERS with a triad color combination of RO, YG, BV; stencil pattern is on page 28

About Color

Hue is another name for color. *Intensity* is the brightness or strength of a pure color, and *value* refers to the darkness or lightness of a color.

Light colors, that is tints, pastels, or pale colors, are usually made by adding a bit of pure color to white. (Adding white to a color usually results in too much paint.) White reduces the brightness or intensity and lessens or subdues the value of the color.

To change the value of a color, add another pure color such as a complementary color. A color added to a color will keep the resulting color fresh. Black added to a color will make it dull, muddy, and lifeless.

Mexican Rose

Photo 1. MEXICAN ROSE (62" x 84") stencil painted and hand quilted by the author

MEXICAN ROSE started out as a true wholecloth quilt, but it lacked personality. The quilt top was cut up and red sashing was inserted. The green leaves were stencil painted with a stenciling prop of a plastic onion bag stretched in an embroidery hoop. This gave the appearance of a printed fabric. Red shark's teeth edging frames the quilt. All the stencil outlines were hand quilted (photo 1).

Placement diagram

Full-sized pattern

(Blue) Pineapple Clusters

Photo 2. (Blue) Pineapple Clusters (32" x 32") stencil painted by the author and machine quilted by Brenda Sheldon

All blue motifs in (Blue) Pineapple Clusters were painted with the aid of a stenciling prop of wire hardware cloth, which produced the effect of a printed fabric. Blue embroidery floss was worked in a chain stitch to define the edges of the sashing strips. Machine quilting follows the stencil outlines and sashing (photo 2).

Theorem Baskets

Photo 3. THEOREM BASKETS (66" x 90") stencil painted and hand quilted by the author

This stencil-painted THEOREM BASKETS design (photo 3) was popular in the 1820s for theorem paintings (usually done on velvet), a favorite subject taught in fashionable schools for young girls. The hand quilting is close and is worked in many sunburst rays that add a rich texture to the quilt.

Paint•a•*Quilt* **Patterns** 　Marie Monteith Sturmer

Full-sized pattern

Full-sized pattern

Photo 4. FRUIT BASKET (21" x 23") painted with the trace and transfer technique and hand quilted by the author

After the trace and transfer work was finished for this FRUIT BASKET quilt top (photo 4), I added one more interesting step. I enjoy watercolor painting and thought it might be fun to explore the "wash" procedure on fabric. Acrylic paints are easily thinned with water. Starting with the leaves, I used a light yellow-green wash within the black transfer lines. The black lines acted somewhat like a barrier restricting the moist paint. Dark green was scrubbed over to give a shadow effect. This method works if the paint is not too wet. An elephant ear sponge applicator cut to a point works well. Pure color highlights the fruit. Black quilting thread was used on the pen outlines, and pink thread for background fabric.

Christmas Spider Plant

Photo 5. Christmas Spider Plant (67" x 67") stencil painted and hand quilted by the author

The outer border design on Christmas Spider Plant (photo 5) is reminiscent of the messy little white flowers produced by the spider plant. Some say the motifs look like bowling ball pins. Stenciling began in the center of the quilt. The omission of a red leaf was an honest mistake and was not discovered until the concentric quilting was well on its way. Black chain stitch outlines are worked with embroidery floss on the edges of the red, stenciled motifs.

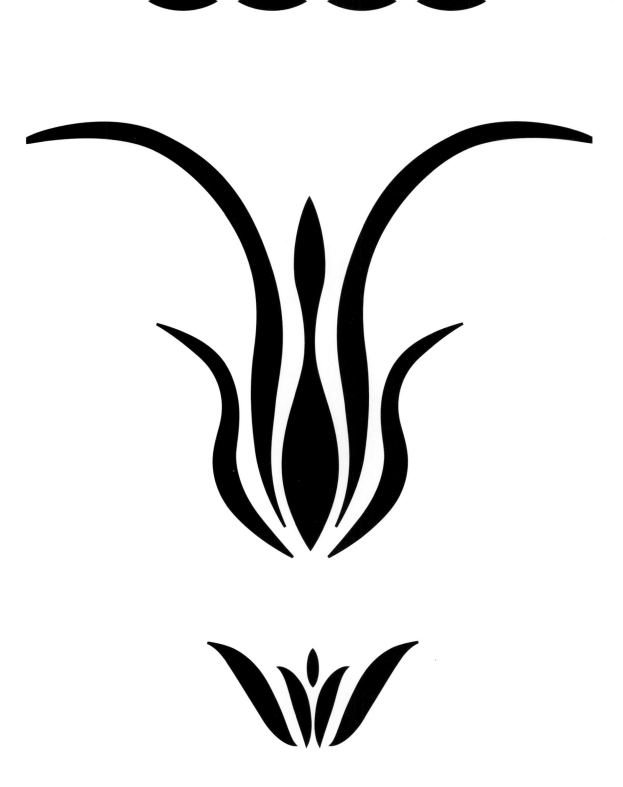

For featured quilt,
enlarge 150%

For featured quilt,
enlarge 400%

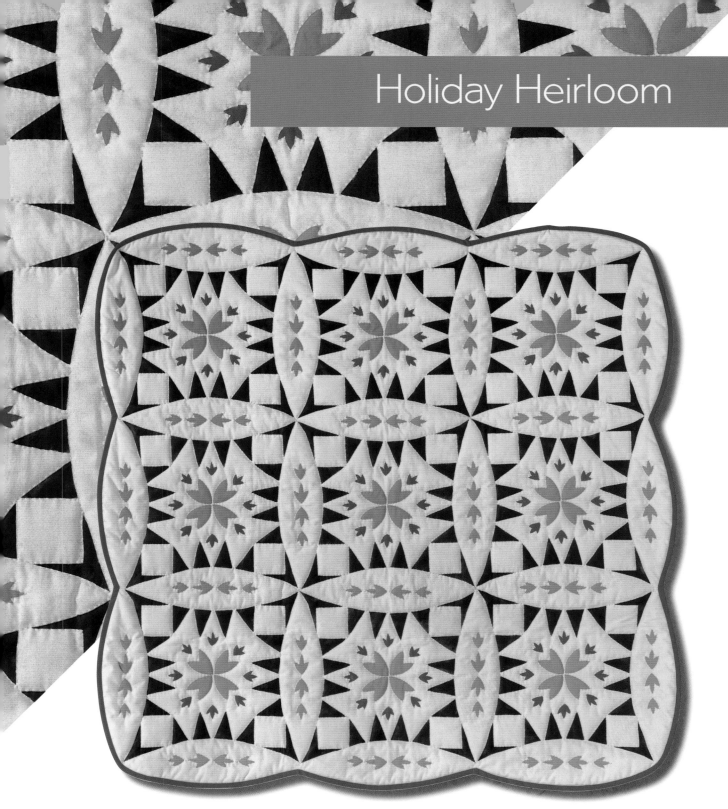

Photo 7. HOLIDAY HEIRLOOM (26" x 26") stencil painted and hand quilted by the author

The stencil-painted design in HOLIDAY HEIRLOOM would fool anyone because it looks just like patchwork (photo 7). All stencil elements are outline quilted. The red quilt binding is a nice repeat of color. The quilt blocks look good on point too (see the Holiday Heirloom floorcloth on page 21).

For featured quilt,
enlarge 200%

Monochromatic Melody

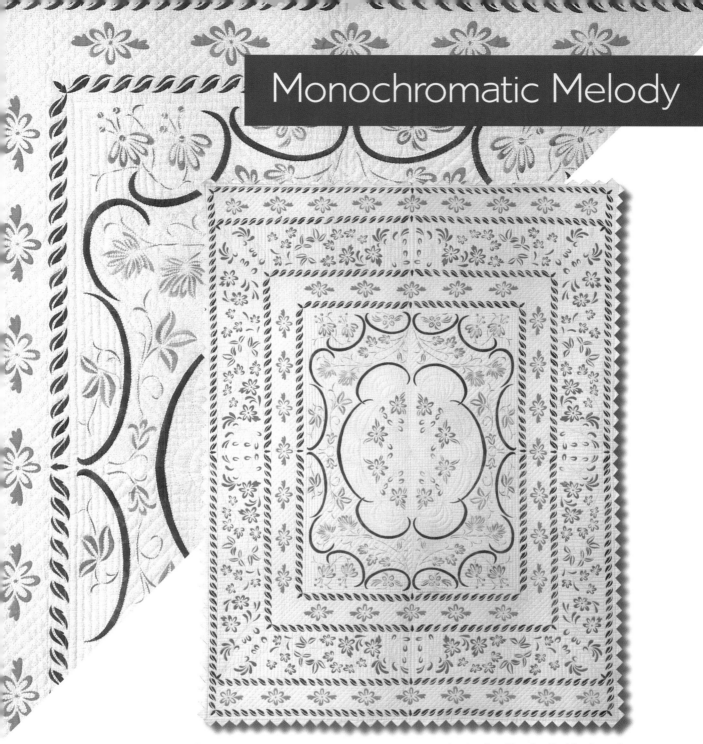

Photo 8. MONOCHROMATIC MELODY (56" x 74") stencil painted and hand quilted by the author

MONOCHROMATIC MELODY (photo 8) was inspired by the monochromatic white-on-white crewel embroidery upholstered fabric on my grandmother's Eastlake settee. The quilt stenciling started in the center and just grew and grew. The flaring baroque lines created a medallion style quilt. I had a general idea what the quilt might look like, but as I went on, new stencils had to be cut to fit in with what I had already painted. The hand quilting is close. All stenciled motifs are outline quilted with white cotton perle worked in a backstitch through to the underside. The textures on both sides are beautiful. Shark's teeth finish the edges.

Full-sized pattern

Paint·a·*Quilt* **Patterns** ✺ Marie Monteith Sturmer

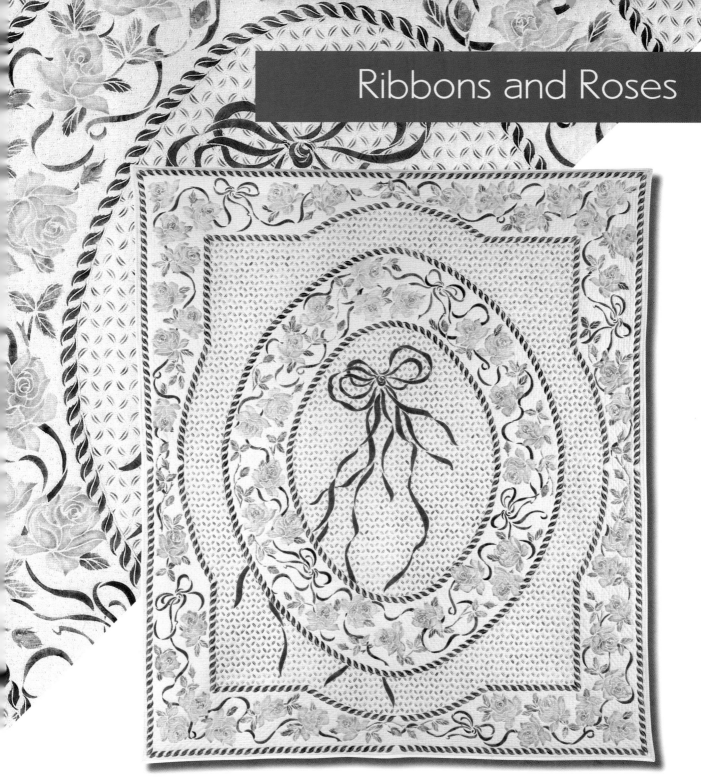

Ribbons and Roses

Photo 9. RIBBONS AND ROSES (72" x 86") stencil painted and hand quilted by the author

In RIBBONS AND ROSES (photo 9), the stencil-painted design of large borders of pink cabbage roses is twined about with green ribbons. The background of the borders is studded with French knots that give it a wonderful textured surface. The background of the quilt is stenciled with a closely stitched series of double Xs. Each stenciled motif is outline quilted. This quilt is in the Founders Collection of the Museum of the American Quilter's Society, Paducah, Kentucky.

Ribbons and Cabbage Roses

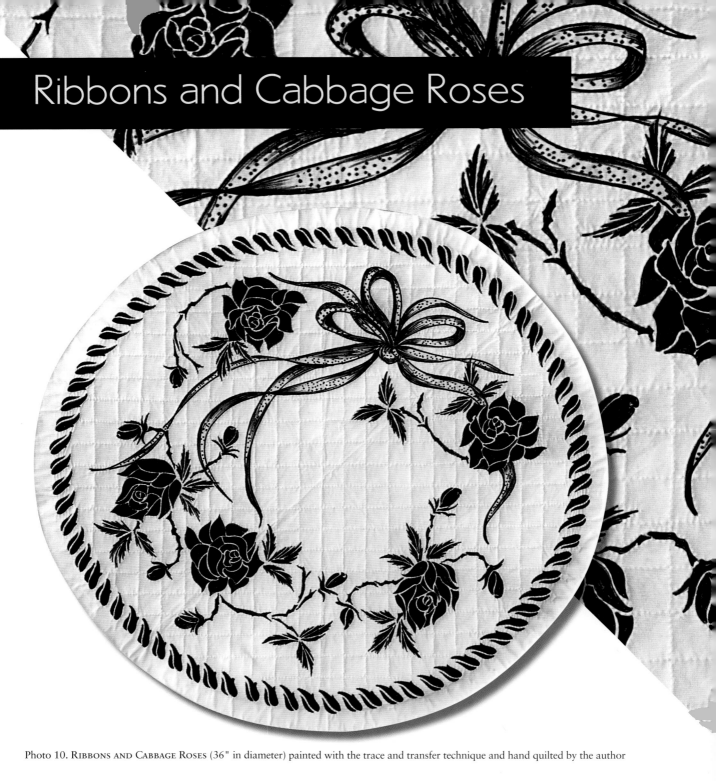

Photo 10. RIBBONS AND CABBAGE ROSES (36" in diameter) painted with the trace and transfer technique and hand quilted by the author

My RIBBONS AND ROSES quilt was the inspiration for the round RIBBONS AND CABBAGE ROSES wall quilt (photo 10). The cabbage roses were drawn from the original stencils copied onto the fabric with the trace and transfer technique. A black permanent felt-tip pen was used instead of paint. Different, but interesting, and it's an easy way to make a contemporary quilt. The quilting was worked with black thread following the transfer drawing lines.

Paint·a·*Quilt* **Patterns**   Marie Monteith Sturmer

Stencil placement

Full-sized pattern

Paint·a·*Quilt* **Patterns** ✦ Marie Monteith Sturmer

Double Wedding Ring

Photo 11. DOUBLE WEDDING RING (32" x 43") stencil painted and hand quilted by the author

The sparse stencil-painted areas in DOUBLE WEDDING RING look like calico fabric (photo 11). They're united by back-stitched embroidery lines. These delineate the ring design. The flower designs are hand quilted. Large areas of white ground fabric in the centers of the rings left room for a fancy quilting pattern.

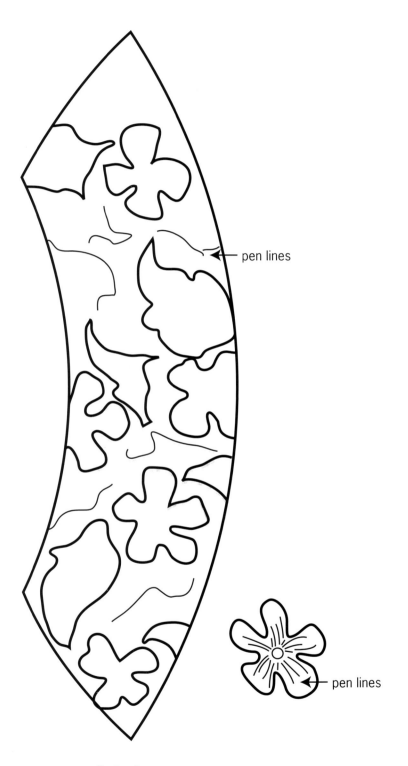

pen lines

pen lines

Full-sized pattern

For featured quilt,
enlarge 200%

Double Rings

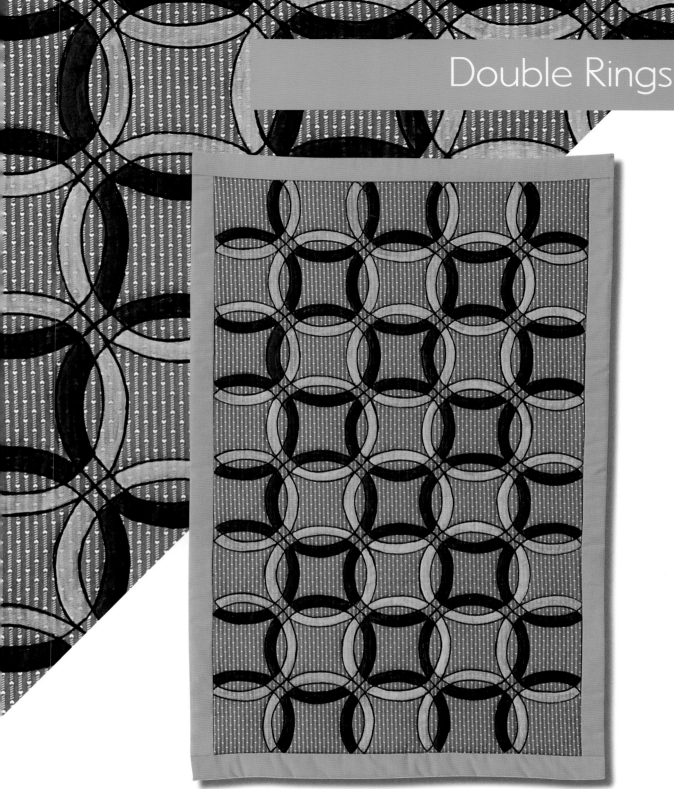

Photo 12. DOUBLE RINGS (20" x 31") painted with the trace and transfer technique and hand quilted by the author

The scale of the trace and transfer pattern on DOUBLE RINGS is much smaller but is still working the same charm (photo 12). The printed background fabric necessitated a second coat of paint on the light green ring. Painted quilts do look good on a printed ground fabric.

Full-sized pattern

Paint·a·*Quilt* **Patterns** ▦ Marie Monteith Sturmer

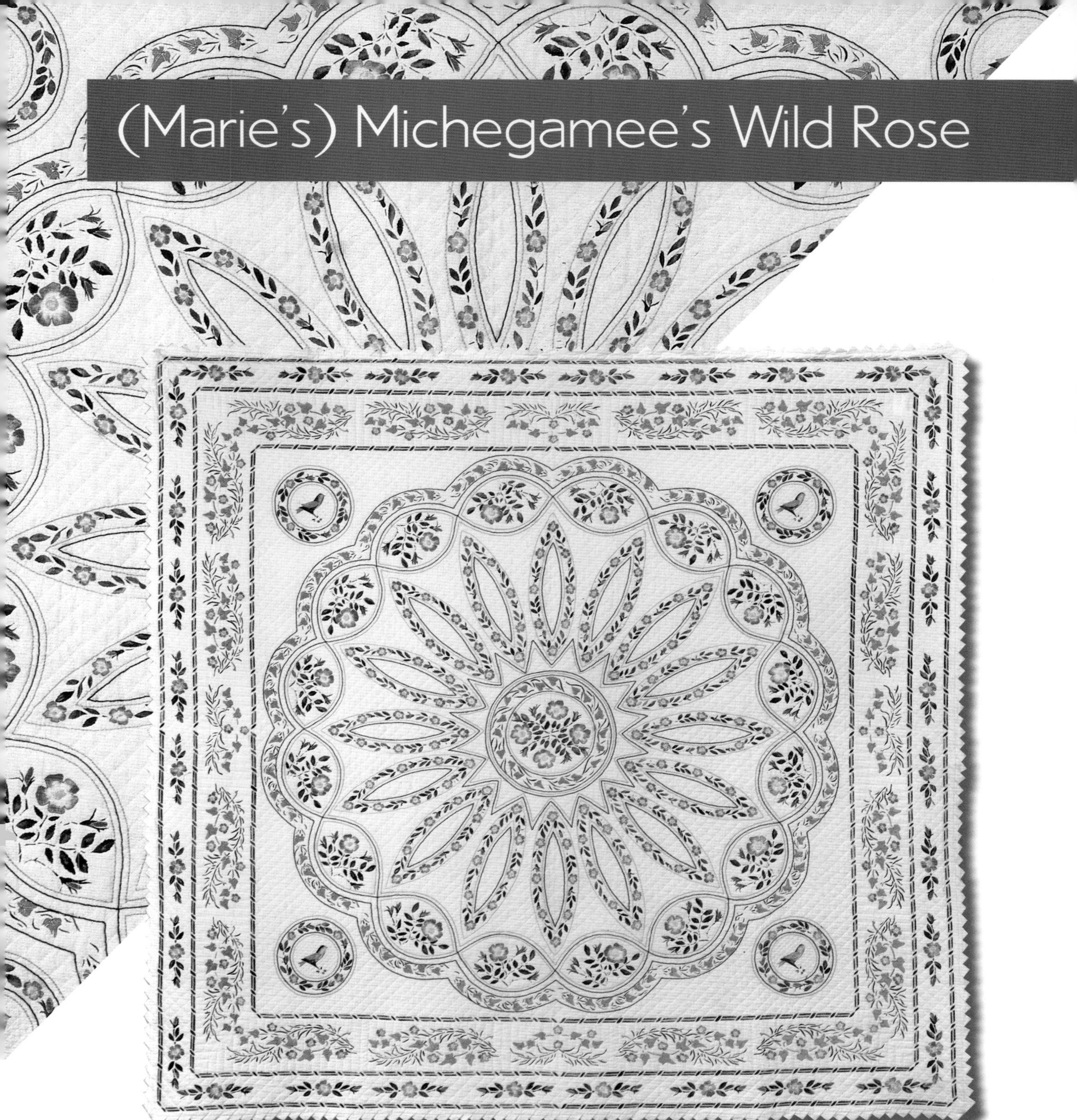

(Marie's) Michegamee's Wild Rose

Photo 13. (Marie's) Michegamee's Wild Rose (72" x 72") stencil painted and hand quilted by the author. (See additional details on this quilt on page 13.) The quilt and pattern are given with permission from the American Folk Art Museum, New York.

I have been inspired many times by my Michegamee's Wild Rose quilt the American Folk Art Museum has in its masterpiece quilt collection. This is a replica I made for myself (photo 13).

Michegamee's Pink and Green

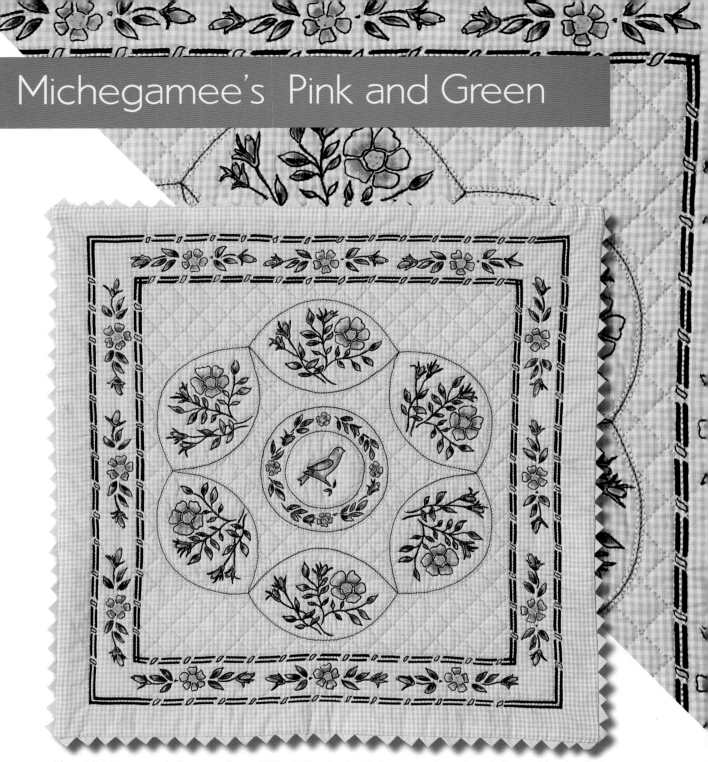

Photo 14. MICHEGAMEE'S PINK AND GREEN (33" x 33") painted with the trace and transfer technique and hand quilted by the author

I used my trace and transfer technique on MICHEGAMEE'S PINK AND GREEN wallhanging (photo 14). The black outlines produced by this method enhance the soft colors. Pink embroidery stitches are worked next to the black lines. The pink shark's teeth edging is fashioned after the inspiration quilt. Black quilting thread was used on all black drawing lines and white thread for background quilting.

Michegamee's Accessories

Photo 15. Placemat, napkins, pillow, and framed motif stencil painted and hand quilted by the author

I used single motifs from the same stencils to make smaller items (photo 15). Using single motifs from complex quilt designs expands the possibilities of stencil quiltmaking.

Circles of Roses

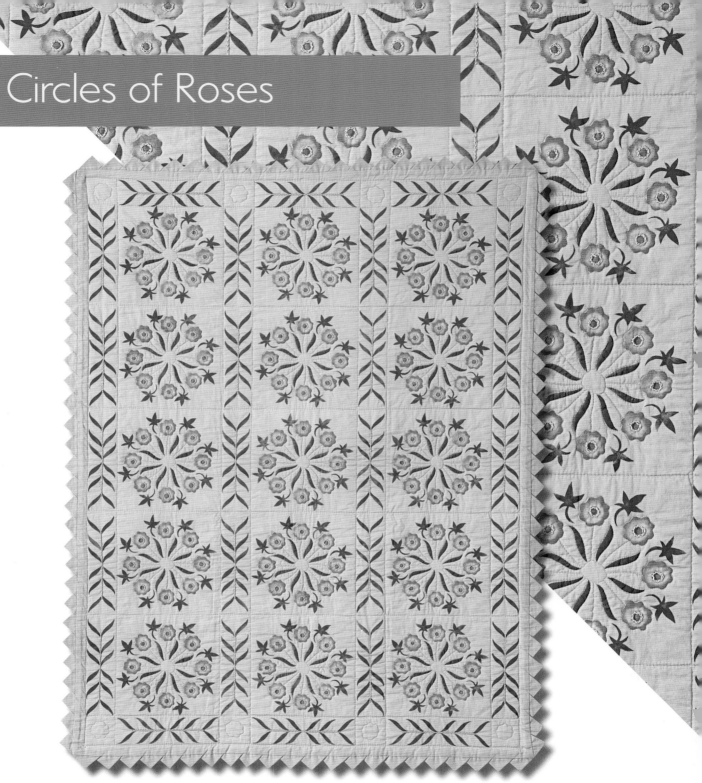

Photo 16. CIRCLES OF ROSES (34" x 46") stencil painted by the author and machine quilted by Brenda Sheldon

Stencil-painted chevron motifs create the sashing and borders of CIRCLES OF ROSES (photo 16). Rows of simple circles, each containing eight roses, are spaced between the sashing. Chain stitches are worked in a circle around each rose with pink embroidery floss. Machine quilting surrounds the roses. Horizontal stitching across the quilt and on either side of the sashing gives the illusion of a pieced quilt. Shark's teeth edging adds to the daintiness of the quilt.

Paint·a·*Quilt* Patterns 🔲 Marie Monteith Sturmer

Purple Flowers

Photo 17. PURPLE FLOWERS (31" x 31") painted with the trace and transfer technique and hand quilted by the author

This PURPLE FLOWERS trace and transfer pastel quilt displays a complementary color scheme of yellow and purple (photo 17). The large flowers were painted by using a prop of a plastic onion bag stretched in an embroidery hoop. The hoop was placed over the flower drawing and painted to show the lines of the plastic as white lines: the results—faux printed fabric. Yellow three-ply yarn worked in a backstitch accents the flower blocks and defines the margin of the quilt.

Jacquard Woven Remnant

Photo 19. JACQUARD WOVEN REMNANT (46" x 46") stencil painted and hand quilted by the author

Most early double-weave Jacquard coverlets were woven by German immigrants living in Pennsylvania. In the 1820s, it was fashionable to have names inscribed on the borders of the coverlets to mark special occasions. The looms were threaded to give a mirror image of the patterns causing the lettering to show in reverse. In JACQUARD WOVEN REMNANT (photo 19), regular quilting thread was lost in the wool fabric, so buttonhole quilting thread was worked with a backstitch and carried to the back of the quilt, giving a unique and beautiful design and texture. The quilt is finished in a self-fringed edge.

For featured quilt,
enlarge 200%

For featured quilt,
enlarge 200%

Photo 21. CIRCLES AND CIRCLES (45" x 45") stencil painted and hand quilted by the author

This wall quilt will keep your eyes busy with circles changing from one to another and back again (photo 21). The quilt is very simple but ever so fascinating. Both red and green stencils were painted through a stenciling prop of a plastic onion bag stretched in an embroidery hoop. The large quilting stitches are worked with red yarn.

For featured quilt,
enlarge 300%

Paint·a·*Quilt* **Patterns**   Marie Monteith Sturmer

Photo 22. Front and back of BIG STITCH (68" x 82") stencil painted and hand quilted by the author. (See additional details about the quilt on page 12.)

The background of BIG STITCH is hand quilted in a small diamond pattern. The outlines of stems and leaves are worked in a backstitch with blue cotton crochet string, which keep the stitches large. The embroidery carries the design to the back of the quilt. The dark red flowers have quilted halos. The shark's teeth edging gives a strong accent (photo 22).

For featured quilt,
enlarge 500%

Paint•a•*Quilt* **Patterns**   Marie Monteith Sturmer

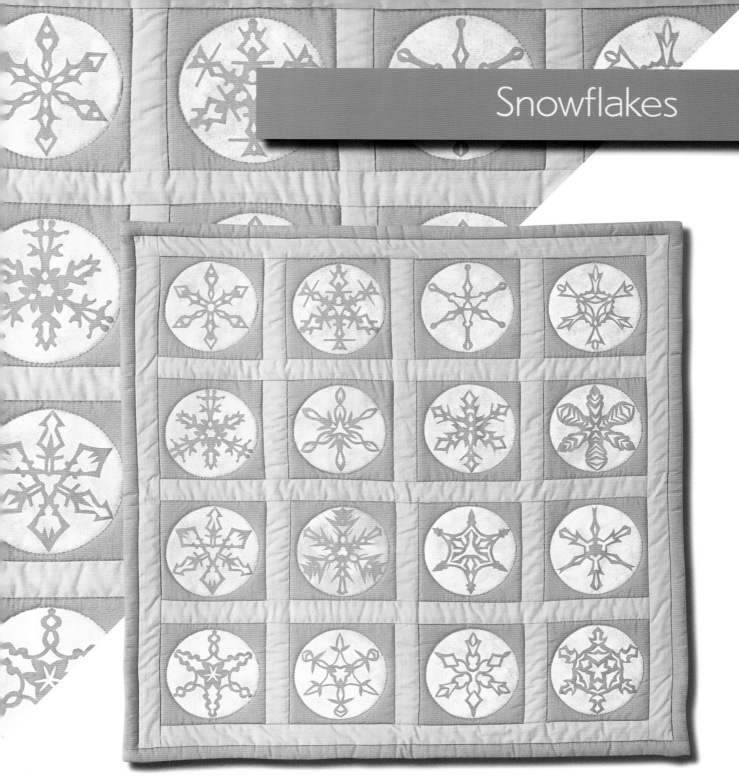

Photo 23. SNOWFLAKES (33"x 33") reverse painted and hand quilted by the author. (See additional details about the quilt on page 15.)

For a six-pointed snowflake, fold a paper square in half. Mark the center point of the fold. Fold the half-square in thirds with the point of the folds meeting at the center mark. Cut the outer edges to form a teepee shape. Cut on the folds and along the outside edges to make the snowflake. Unfold carefully.

Laurel Rose

Photo 24. LAUREL ROSE (63" x 84") stencil painted and hand quilted by the author. (See additional details about the quilt on page 12.)

For featured quilt,
enlarge 400%

For featured quilt,
enlarge 200%

Paint·a·*Quilt* **Patterns**   Marie Monteith Sturmer

Photo 25. BALTIMORE-STYLE ALBUM (71" x 82") stencil painted and hand quilted by the author. (See additional details about the quilt on page 13.)

For featured quilt,
enlarge 200%

Paint·a·**Quilt** **Patterns** Marie Monteith Sturmer

For featured quilt,
enlarge 200%

Paint·a·*Quilt* **Patterns** ◼ Marie Monteith Sturmer

For featured quilt,
enlarge 200%

For featured quilt,
enlarge 200%

Paint·a·*Quilt* **Patterns**   Marie Monteith Sturmer

For featured quilt,
enlarge 200%

Paint•a•*Quilt* **Patterns**   Marie Monteith Sturmer

Carolina Lily

Photo 26. CAROLINA LILY (43" x 43") stencil painted and hand quilted by the author. (See additional details on this quilt on page 13.)

Placement diagram

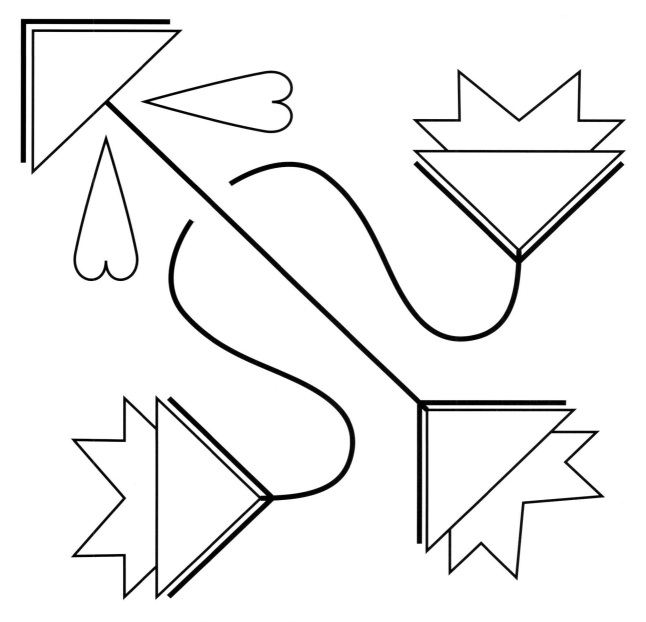

Strawberries to Eat

Photo 27. STRAWBERRIES TO EAT (23" x 36") painted with the trace and transfer technique and hand quilted by the author. (See additional details on this quilt on page 16.)

For featured quilt,
enlarge 200%

Rob Peter to Pay Paul

Photo 29. ROB PETER TO PAY PAUL (24" x 36") floorcloth stencil painted by the author

Paint·a·*Quilt* **Patterns** ⬚ Marie Monteith Sturmer

For featured floorcloth,
enlarge 200%

Rose Sprigs

Photo 30. ROSE SPRIGS (24" x 36") floorcloth stencil painted by the author

Full-sized pattern

Full-sized pattern

Paint·a·*Quilt* **Patterns** ◼ Marie Monteith Sturmer

Resources

Stencil Artisans League, Inc.
www.sali.org

Stencil Ease
www.stencilease.com
Manufacturer of stencils, paints, brushes, and
accessories including 12" x 18" sheets of 4 mil
Stencil Matte for cutting your own stencils

Dharma Trading Company
www.dharmatrading.com
Fiber art supplies including stenciling paint
and brushes

Bibliography

Bishop, Adele and Cile Lord. *The Art of Decorative Stenciling*. New York: Penguin, 1985.

Bishop, Robert and Carter Houch. *All Flags Flying: American Patriotic Quilts as Expressions of Liberty*. New York: Random House Value Publishing, 1990.

Bishop, Robert. *New Discoveries in American Quilts*. New York: E. P. Dutton, 1975

Gauss, Jane with the Artists and Designers of the Stencil Artisans League, Inc. *Stenciling Techniques: A Complete Guide to Traditional and Contemporary Designs for the Home*. New York: Watson-Guptill Publications, 1995.

Hargrave, Harriet. *Heirloom Machine Quilting, 4th Edition: Comprehensive Guide to Hand-Quilting Effects Using Your Sewing Machine*. Concord, CA: C&T Publishing, 2004.

Jones, Owen and Maxine Lewis (editor). *The Grammar of Ornament*. London: Dorling Kindersley Limited, 2001.

Marhoefer, Barbara, Alice B. Fjelstul, and Patricia B. Schad. *More Early American Stencils in Color*. New York: Dutton Books, 1986

Oliver, Celia. *55 Famous Quilts from the Shelburne Museum in Full Color*. New York: Dover Publications, Inc., 1990.

Spargo, Gillie. *The Step by Step Art of Stenciling*. Emmaus, PA: The JG Press, Inc., 1996.

Safford, Carleton L. and Robert Bishop. *America's Quilts and Coverlets*. New York: Random House Value Publishing (reprint edition), 1987.

Waring, Janet. *Early American Stencils on Walls and Furniture*. New York: Dover Publications, Inc., 1968.

Warren, Elizabeth V. and Sharon L. Eisenstat. *Glorious American Quilts: The Quilt Collection of the Museum of American Folk Art*. New York: Penguin Studio, 1996.

A former art teacher, Marie Sturmer began her art training at Cranbrook Art Academy in Bloomfield Hills, Michigan. She received a bachelor of arts degree with a secondary teaching certificate from Alma College in Michigan and a master of fine arts from Wayne State University in Detroit.

Marie has taught art at the elementary, secondary, and adult levels and spent five years as art department head at a Michigan high school. She has participated in children's art programs on live television and has served as critic teacher for college undergraduate art students at many schools.

Marie is a member of the Stencil Artisans League, Inc., an international, non-profit organization. Through its certification program, Marie has earned both certified stenciler and certified stenciling teacher certifications.

A professional quilter, Marie's forte is stenciling. Her quilts are truly created with an American folk art technique of the 1820s. The *Early American Life* magazine has chosen Marie three times as one of the top 200 traditional craftsmen.

In 1991, she was one of the 25 winners in the *Quilts from America's Flower Garden* contest, sponsored by the Museum of American Folk Art in conjunction with the Great American Quilt Festival in New York City. The museum purchased her quilt MICHEGAMMEE'S WILD ROSE for its permanent collection. Another of her quilts, RIBBONS AND ROSES, was purchased by the Museum of the American Quilter's Society of Paducah, Kentucky, for its Founders Collection.

Marie is the author of *Making a Stenciled ABC Quilt, Stenciled Quilts,* and *Stenciled Quilts for Christmas.* She and husband, son, daughter-in-law, and two grandchildren all live in the village of Lake Ann, Michigan.

Other AQS Books!

This is only a small selection of the books available from the American Quilter's Society. AQS books are known worldwide for timely topics, clear writing, beautiful color photos, and accurate illustrations and patterns. The following books are available from your local bookseller, quilt shop, or public library.

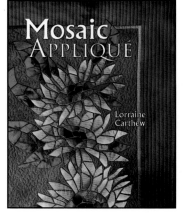

#7071   us$24.95

#6896   us$22.95

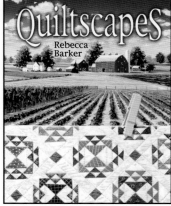

#6204   us$19.95

#7073   us$24.95

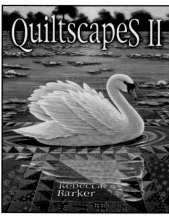
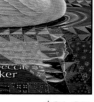

#6680   us$21.95

#6904   us$21.95

#7078   us$24.95

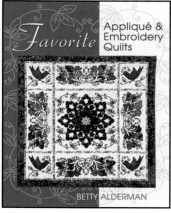

#6410   us$19.95

#7010   us$21.95

Look for these books nationally.
Call or **Visit** our Web site at

1-800-626-5420
www.AmericanQuilter.com